Most Extreme Vacations

Sue Harper • Bonnie Sheppard

Series Editor
Jeffrey D. Wilhelm

Much thought, debate, and research went into choosing and ranking the 10 items in each book in this series. We realize that everyone has his or her own opinion of what is most significant, revolutionary, amazing, deadly, and so on. As you read, you may agree with our choices, or you may be surprised — and that's the way it should be!

an imprint of
■SCHOLASTIC
www.scholastic.com/librarypublishing

A Rubicon book published in association with Scholastic Inc.

Ru'bicon © 2008 Rubicon Publishing Inc.
www.rubiconpublishing.com

is a trademark of The 10 Books

Associate Publishers: Kim Koh, Miriam Bardswich
Project Editor: Amy Land
Editorial Assistant: Jessica Rose
Creative Director: Jennifer Drew
Project Manager/Designer: Jeanette MacLean
Graphic Designer: Waseem Bashar

The publisher gratefully acknowledges the following for permission to reprint copyrighted material in this book.

Every reasonable effort has been made to trace the owners of copyrighted material and to make due acknowledgment. Any errors or omissions drawn to our attention will be gladly rectified in future editions.

"Dangerous Waters" excerpt from "Face to Face with a Monster from the Deep" by Simon Reeve. From *The Observer*, 2006. Copyright Guardian News & Media Ltd.

"Lair of the Leopards" (excerpt) by Yvette Cardozo. From *Diver*, 2003. Reprinted with permission of author.

"Anousheh Ansari Space Blog" (excerpt) by Anousheh Ansari. From Xprize Foundation, www.xprize.org, permission courtesy of Xprize.

Cover: Mountain climber–Getty Images/Stone/David Trood

Library and Archives Canada Cataloguing in Publication

Harper, Suzanne
    The 10 most extreme vacations / Sue Harper and Bonnie Sheppard.

Includes index.
ISBN 978-1-55448-534-5

    1. Readers (Elementary). 2. Readers—Vacations. I. Sheppard, Bonnie II. Title. III. Title: Ten most extreme vacations.

PE1117.H3893 2007a   428.6   C2007-906688-7

1 2 3 4 5 6 7 8 9 10   10   17 16 15 14 13 12 11 10 09 08

Printed in Singapore

Contents

14

18

38

LIVING ON THE EDGE

Note: The activities in this book require skills and training with the help of professionals. Do not attempt to try any of these extreme sports on your own or with your friends.

HIKER—CARSTEN PETER/NATIONAL GEOGRAPHIC/GETTY IMAGES

If money were not a problem, and you had all the time in the world, where would you go for a vacation? Would you go on a luxury cruise in the Mediterranean, lie on the beach in Hawaii, or visit the Great Wall of China? Or would you choose an extreme vacation, one that leaves your palms sweating, your heart thumping, and your family chewing their nails until your safe return?

These are the kinds of trips people react to by saying, "You're going to do WHAT?!" Most people wouldn't do these things if they were forced, let alone for fun. But to the true adventure seeker, there is nothing like the satisfaction that comes from taking on a challenge and succeeding.

In this book, we present our choice of the 10 most extreme vacations. In ranking them, we considered these criteria: How remote were the locations? How challenging were the weather, environment, and terrain? What skills, training, and physical fitness were required? What equipment and gear were essential? What safety measures were in place?

As you read, consider the dangers and risks involved in these vacations. Ask yourself:

WHAT MAKES A VACATION EXTREME?

terrain: *physical features of an area of land.*

To avoid serious injuries, students at a rodeo school are required to wear proper safety gear and to learn the proper way to fall from a bull.

OL

WHERE IN THE WORLD? All over the world, including in the United States

WOW FACTOR: You will learn to sit on a bucking bull, and try to stay on its back for at least eight seconds.

Think school is tough? Try signing up for rodeo school! Instead of sitting at your desk you'll be climbing on top of an unruly bull, which can weigh more than 1,300 pounds, while it kicks and lunges beneath you. Get ready to hang on tight!

Even if you've never been face-to-face with one of these beasts before, you can still sign up for this school. Your teachers will train you on mechanical equipment first. Only after you've tried on some championship-level gear and learned some difficult techniques will you have to face the real thing.

Some bulls may be quiet at first, but they are NOT interested in giving you a smooth ride. They just want you off their backs — the sooner, the better.

Get ready for a bumpy ride!

RODEO SCHOOL

GETTING THERE

Do you think you're brave enough to challenge a bucking bull? If you do, you can choose from a number of vacation destinations. You can find rodeo schools all over the United States, especially in the Southwest. You'll even get to live on an authentic ranch while you're there.

? Look at the picture below — particularly how the cowboy is dressed. What other protective gear do you think he should wear?

GEARING UP

If you want to ride with the pros, you'll need some impressive gear. Rubber-soled sneakers won't make the cut. You will need a sturdy pair of cowboy boots with special heels to keep your spurs from moving around. The school will lend you protective vests, chaps, gloves, and special safety gear.

THRILL OF A LIFETIME

This isn't your typical classroom. Riders need to be physically fit and willing to take risks. Most rodeo schools are three days long. On your first morning you will learn techniques, watch professionals, and go through drills and practices. By the afternoon, you will meet your first bull. Some schools offer programs for younger riders, who can try to stay on top of a small bull, a steer, or a calf.

spurs: *spiked wheels on boots used to urge an animal forward*

? What questions would you want to ask a professional bull rider before you sign up for rodeo school?

A bucking bull will lunge and kick to get you off its back.

Quick Fact

Some people practice on a mechanical bull before they sign up for rodeo school. It might be your safest bet. The U.S. professional rodeo circuit averages one or two deaths per year in rodeo-related accidents.

10   9   8   7   6

BETTER SAFE THAN SORRY

BULL RIDING IS AN EXTREME SPORT WITH SOME EXTREME RISKS! READ THE FOLLOWING CHART TO LEARN HOW RIDERS CAN PROTECT THEMSELVES FROM GETTING HURT.

INJURIES	GEAR
• INTERNAL INJURIES	**PROTECTIVE VEST** • made of Kevlar, a light, but very strong fiber that absorbs the shock of the fall
• LOSS OF TEETH	**MOUTHGUARD** • like many athletes, bull riders wear mouthguards to prevent their teeth from being knocked out
• ROPE BURN	**LEATHER GLOVE** • worn on the hand that holds the rope
• HEAD AND FACE INJURIES	**COWBOY HAT** • provides the lowest level of protection from strong hooves or horns **SAFETY HELMET AND FACE MASK** • provides the most protection, but many riders claim that their vision is restricted
• PUNCTURES AND CUTS	**CHAPS** • help bull riders to avoid the types of injuries sustained when they are kicked, stepped on, or butted by horns
• SPRAINS	**BOOTS** • protect the ankles and feet and provide protection for the lower leg **TAPE** • ankles, wrists, elbows, and knees can all be wrapped with tape prior to the ride

The Expert Says...

"It's just instant power. [The bull's] first move out of the gate is so much mass, and it's so quick. It's weird, and it's scary ... because you know you can die."

— Jeff Fraley, bull-riding school participant and director of *Bull Riders: Chasing the Dream*

Take Note

This extreme vacation charges in at #10 on our list. Though professionals take great care to teach the essential skills and provide safety equipment, it's still a risky ride!
• What do you think makes some people crave this kind of adventure?

5   4   3   2   1

The Sami people of Norway have been reindeer herders for thousands of years. If you think vacations should mean no work and all play, then don't sign up for this extreme trip!

RDING

WOW FACTOR: It's dangerous terrain, harsh cold weather, and little sleep!

A trip to Norway to herd a large group of wild reindeer doesn't sound too extreme, does it? Think again! As if sub-zero temperatures weren't bad enough, these reindeer-herding grounds are found at the remote northern tip of Norway. If anything goes wrong, you'll be miles away from the nearest hospital.

You won't just be along for the ride on this vacation. You will be expected to work alongside the Sami people of Norway, as if you were one of them. Just think of it as a lesson in extreme winter camping, with a twist! Get ready for some difficult physical labor and very little sleep.

Despite the risks, tourists come to Norway for the beautiful landscape and the chance to live with wild reindeer. Activities can include moving reindeer from one place to another, lasso throwing, and branding the animals. Also, you might be asked to participate in *joiking* (pronounced yoik-ing). This is the vocal tradition of the Sami people, somewhat like singing. You can join them in one of these ancient chants.

REINDEER HERDING

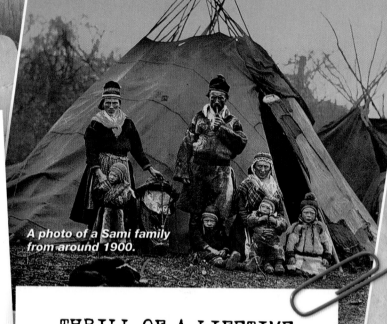

A photo of a Sami family from around 1900.

GETTING THERE

To take part in this extreme vacation, you'd better be physically fit! The Sami people are nomads, who live in tents and move around from place to place. You'll need to keep up! While some of the uneven and dangerous terrain is accessible by snowmobile, much of your trip will be on foot. Lack of sleep and eating only what you can carry will be challenging for you, no matter how fit you are.

GEARING UP

This is your chance to escape from the modern world. You will need to carry all your supplies on your snowmobile and your *pulk* (sled). When you stop for the night, you will need to help to build your *lavvu* (tents), which are much like North American teepees. Don't expect a bed or a camp cot! A good sleeping bag will be all you have to keep you warm.

? What supplies would you take on the trip if you could only bring a backpack?

THRILL OF A LIFETIME

Many of the traditions of the Sami people have been built on a long history of herding reindeer. This includes wearing reindeer skins, eating reindeer meat, and using reindeer bones as tools. Make sure you try the *renkok*, a traditional reindeer stew! Bundle up, and pack your sled! This is a trip that you'll never forget.

? What would you enjoy most on a trip like this one?

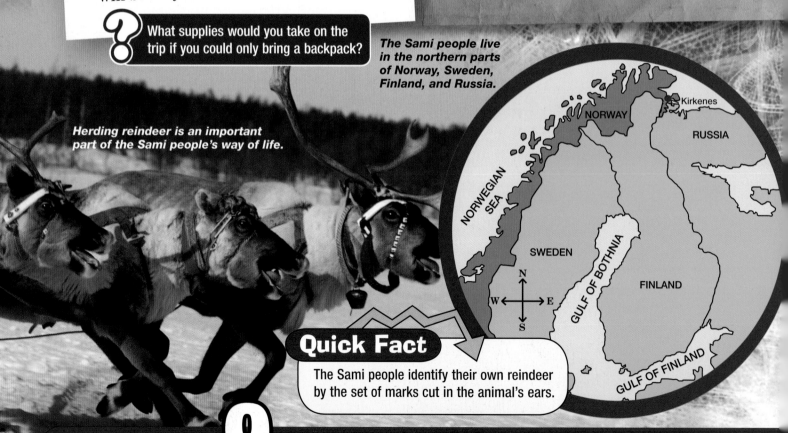

Herding reindeer is an important part of the Sami people's way of life.

The Sami people live in the northern parts of Norway, Sweden, Finland, and Russia.

Quick Fact

The Sami people identify their own reindeer by the set of marks cut in the animal's ears.

10   9   8   7   6

DISAPPEARING LAND

The Sami people have relied on herding reindeer for generations. This fact chart explains why their traditional way of life might be in danger.

A sled will be your best mode of transportation on this journey.

LOGGING

Cutting down trees in Norway's forests can cause problems for reindeer. They often move between feeding grounds, looking for tasty food. Much of their diet can be found in the forests of Norway. As trees are destroyed, reindeer risk losing important grazing lands. This could cause them to starve to death.

POWER

In order to bring electricity to houses in the area, power lines have been built. This has forced reindeer to leave their grazing lands because there is no longer enough room or food for them to survive.

MILITARY

Northern Norway is one of the few locations in Europe where low-level flight training can be conducted. NATO (North Atlantic Treaty Organization) has also proposed testing missile systems in the area. Training and testing would mean loud explosions and noises, which would frighten the reindeer away.

MINING

Many parts of the traditional herding lands of the Sami are rich in minerals. Some companies think this makes them a perfect spot for mining. This would leave herds homeless.

The Expert Says...

" Some 45,000 Sami still live in Norway, but only a fraction — about 1,500 — still carry out traditional tasks of reindeer herding. "

— Gary Tischler, journalist for *The Washington Times*

Take Note

While you don't have to ride on a bucking bull, this extreme trip stands at #9 because it lasts longer, and you have to travel to a very isolated location and put up with hard physical work with little food and sleep.
• How do you think the lives of the Sami people would change without reindeer herding? Explain.

5   4   3   2   1

8 SURFING THE

Tidal bores like the pororoca occur in only 100 rivers in the world. Since 1997, the world's best surfers have traveled to Brazil to ride these waves.

POROROCA

WHERE IN THE WORLD? The Rio Araguari in Central Brazil

WOW FACTOR: One wave can last up to 45 minutes — but most surfers can't stay on their boards that long!

Do you have what it takes to climb on top of a surfboard and ride a violent wave? This 12-foot wall of water might be the least of your worries. In these turbulent waters you'll put yourself at risk of becoming lunch for a group of piranhas or an alligator. Plus, while in the jungles of Brazil, you'll need to watch out for poisonous snakes, scorpions, and even jaguars!

The *pororoca* is a tidal bore that is formed as the incoming Atlantic tide collides with and overpowers the outflowing river. Chances are you will hear it before you see it coming. Tupi Indians call this monstrous wave the *poroc-poroc*, meaning "the great roar." One surfer compared the enormous sound to the rumble of an oncoming train.

When the mighty wave rushes toward you, get ready to jump. Just don't think too hard about what may be floating around beneath you. Here it comes! Get ready to surf the pororoca!

tidal bore: *wave that travels upstream from an ocean into a river*

SURFING THE POROROCA

SURINAME
GUYANA
FRENCH GUIANA
Rio Araguari
ATLANTIC OCEAN
Amazon River
BRAZIL

GETTING THERE

Before attacking the pororoca, you will need to spend a few days at a camp in Macapá. Sounds relaxing? Don't be so sure! The weather here is so hot that tourists often need a few days just to get used to the weather before doing anything too tiring, like surfing. Next, you will spend at least four hours driving down a muddy road to get to your surfing destination. Make sure to get there early, in order to catch the tide at around 6:00 AM. These waves don't come often, so you'd better not sleep in.

GEARING UP

Your surfboard is a must. The type of gear you need is not sold locally. You will probably want to bring a very tight-fitting swimsuit made from spandex or Lycra. The candirú, a small fish, can swim up a person's pant legs, dig in with its spines, and feast on its host's blood. The fish can only be removed by surgery. Wearing baggy shorts, no matter how fashionable, is asking for trouble.

? Why do you think some travelers are willing to risk their lives for the chance to surf this dangerous wave?

THRILL OF A LIFETIME

You must wait for just the right moment to mount your board. If you miss this wave, you might have to wait a few hours before another one comes along. That's a long time to sit around waiting, knowing that there could be piranhas and poisonous snakes below you. Unlike reindeer herding, you don't have efficient guides like the Sami to ensure you get to where you want to go. The wave is in complete control. This extreme vacation is like a roller coaster — without the seatbelts!

? How is this extreme sport like a roller coaster? How does it differ?

Watch out for piranhas and snakes while surfing the pororoca.

Quick Fact

The pororoca is strongest during the rainy season in March and April. The tidal bores, which appear every 12 hours for several days, are at their highest.

10   9   **8**   7   6

DANGEROUS WATERS

Simon Reeve has traveled around the world riding the surf. In this excerpt from his first-person account, he describes his meeting with the pororoca.

From "Face to Face with a Monster from the Deep," by Simon Reeve, *The Observer*, September 3, 2006.

As they prepared to jump into the water, Stanley [Simon's guide] and Edjiman [Stanley's surfer friend] seemed surprisingly calm.

"All or nothing," said Edjiman, "if you miss it the dream is over." Both surfers gripped their boards, leapt out of each boat and began to paddle away from the wave. Within seconds the surf had caught and swallowed them whole, but then I spotted Edjiman's head at the base of the wave, clinging desperately to his surfboard as the wave raged around him. Then Stanley appeared [160 feet] away. … The two of them were clinging on for dear life.

Edjiman held on bravely for five minutes before vanishing into the surf. Despite the force of the water, Stanley skillfully moved his board to a calmer patch of wave and then clambered to his feet.

We cheered and hollered as Stanley made a few flash moves, then slipped backward off his board to be devoured by the wave. Then it was my turn.

After leaping into the water I turned away from the wave, then tried to paddle quickly to build up some speed. But I was too slow: I glanced over my shoulder to see the huge wave engulfing me from behind. As I took a deep breath and kicked my legs hard, the muddy wave roared over the top of me and sucked me backward into darkness. I rolled over and over in the water … then the angry wave ejected me and I floated to the surface.

"Congratulations, you surfed the pororoca," said Stanley, after hauling me into the rescue boat. I looked at him in amazement. How could anyone describe my moment in the water as "surfing"? … I realized surfing the pororoca was less about standing up, and more about being prepared to surrender control to a vicious wave and take a chance in the dark waters of the [Rio] Araguari.

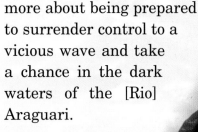

The Expert Says…

"The wave is very powerful and can destroy anything — trees, local houses, islands … and sweeps up wild animals, like snakes — the anaconda — alligators, spiders, piranhas, and even jaguars.

— Serginho Laus, professional Brazilian surfer and journalist

Take Note

This extreme ride sweeps into the #8 spot. It is dangerous, putting surfers at risk of a concussion or even drowning. Like reindeer herding, travelers have to get adjusted to the extreme weather conditions.
• Compare the extreme climates that tourists face in Norway to the Rio Araguari. Which do you think is riskier to the tourists? Explain.

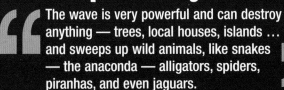

5   4   3   2   1

EXPLORING A

An active volcano, unlike a dormant one, is more likely to erupt. Exploring an active volcano has many risks.

MOUNT MARUM VOLCANO–CARSTEN PETER/NATIONAL GEOGRAPHIC

VOLCANO

WOW FACTOR: Extreme heat and weather conditions are nothing compared to the risk of a potential eruption!

Have you ever thought about outrunning a stream of scalding hot lava? Well, if you've made the decision to explore an active volcano, you'd better be prepared. Even if the chances of a major eruption are slim, you still have to worry about getting lost, suffering from altitude sickness, and struggling along on unstable terrain.

For this adventure, you will travel to Ambrym, a tiny island in the middle of the South Pacific. The last major eruption on the island took place in 1913, killing hundreds. But today, Ambrym's Mount Marum and Mount Benbow still ooze with ash and lava as the result of minor eruptions.

The mixture of sulfur and chlorine gases belching out of a volcano's vents mixed with the regular rainfall forms an acid that can wear away anything metal, including watches and cameras. Don't even think about what that can do to your skin!

EXPLORING A VOLCANO

A satellite view of a volcano on Ambrym Island

GETTING THERE

Climbing these volcanoes takes energy and strength. Some trekking experience is highly recommended. To reach the top, you will climb through thick, lush jungle that is often difficult to navigate. Don't expect to stay at a fancy hotel on this vacation! Your accommodation on the volcano is basic. It is made up of little more than tents and sleeping bags.

? What are some activities you could do to prepare for this trip?

GEARING UP

Make sure to pack lightly. You'll need to fit everything for this extreme vacation into your backpack. Bring along a hard hat, maps, a compass, and enough food and water. Don't forget to bring appropriate clothing, including climbing shoes and gloves. Unless you want to sleep outside, surrounded by the ash of the volcano, you will need a heavy-duty tent.

trekking: *making a slow and difficult journey*

THRILL OF A LIFETIME

For the most daring tourists, a vacation to a volcano's tip is not complete without taking a look inside. The lava, bubbling almost 1,000 feet within Mount Marum, gurgles and hypnotizes all who gaze in. Professionals can even dangle inside the volcano's craters, hanging by a single rope. Stop by the spectacular lava lakes, where bright red and orange molten lava pops and bubbles on the surface. Just don't get too close!

molten: *liquified by heat*

A breathing device like this one is needed for this journey.

Quick Fact

Even volcanoes that have not erupted in 500 years can suddenly erupt. On May 18, 1980, Mount St. Helens erupted in Washington State after more than 100 years of inactivity. The explosion killed approximately 60 people and caused $1.2 billion in damages.

? Do you think active volcanoes should be turned into tourist spots? Why?

Ambrym by the Numbers

You might want to check out this **list** before heading to Ambrym!

5 the number of hours it takes to hike to a base camp from your hotel

7 the number of miles across the field of ash covering Ambrym

50 the wind speed in miles near the Niri Taten crater of Mount Marum

2,200 the temperature in degrees Fahrenheit of the lava in the volcanoes of Ambrym

4,167 the height in feet of Ambrym's largest volcano, Mount Marum

7,000 the cost in *vatu* (about US $70) of an overnight trek in Ambrym

A volcano's lava is made of liquefied rock.

The Expert Says...

"Every few minutes huge molten blobs seem to soar in slow motion. A second or two later a noise from beneath the Earth — a rumbling booooom — fills the pit … It's mesmerizing."

— Donovan Webster, journalist for *National Geographic*

Take Note

Like the pororoca, the volcanoes of Ambrym are natural phenomena. The pororoca comes twice a day at a predictable time. An active volcano can erupt at any time, without warning! The danger of getting lost or hurt on this extreme hike places this vacation at #7 on our list.

• Where would you rather go — to surf the pororoca or to Ambrym? Explain your choice.

5   4   3   2   1

6 BACKCOUNTRY

Backcountry skiing means flying down icy, unmarked slopes, in areas where few skiers have ever dared to ski.

MOUNT DAMAVAND—CORBIS; SKIER—ISTOCKPHOTO

SKIING

WHERE IN THE WORLD? On Mount Damavand, which is located in the Alborz mountain range in Iran

WOW FACTOR: At an altitude of 18,600 feet, even the best skiers will think twice before skiing down Mount Damavand!

Iran, like most of the Middle East, is known for scorching-hot deserts. But in fact, Iran also has some of the most amazing ski hills in the world — and some of the most extreme.

Mount Damavand isn't your ordinary ski mountain. You'll be sliding down 9,800 near-vertical feet of untracked snow. This kind of skiing in a remote location, where few others have dared to ski, is known as backcountry skiing. One wrong move and your skiing days could be over forever!

If you're not used to high altitude, this extreme vacation could be deadly. The simple act of breathing is difficult in the thin air at the top of this enormous extinct volcano.

If you think that you're brave enough, grab your skis. You're about to ski down some of the world's most dangerous terrain, while fighting against extreme weather conditions.

---

extinct: *no longer active; cannot erupt anymore*

BACKCOUNTRY SKIING

Top view of Mount Damavand, overlooking the crater

GETTING THERE

Before you go to Iran, you will need a visitor's visa, which is neither easy nor quick to get. Once you get to the base of Mount Damavand, don't expect a leisurely ride up a chairlift. The only way to get to where you are going is to use your legs. You will need to trek for two or three days with all of your ski equipment and your climbing gear on your back. During the climb to the summit of Mount Damavand, you will be sleeping in shelters that range from well-equipped cabins to primitive huts.

GEARING UP

Training for this vacation is very important. Plenty of hiking, skiing, and biking will get you into shape. Once in Iran, you will have to spend at least three days getting acclimatized to the altitude. Most people do this by skiing at Dizin, a local ski resort. Pack lightly. You will need safety gear, such as flares and shovels, along with your skis and food supplies.

---

visa: *permit allowing a visitor to enter a country*
acclimatized: *used to environmental or climatic changes*

THRILL OF A LIFETIME

Even if you are an experienced skier, you can't control the severe weather conditions. Pay attention to the weather forecast so you don't get caught in high winds or an unexpected blizzard. Most climbers go through avalanche training, which teaches them how to react to a roaring downfall of snow. This training might just pay off when skiing in Iran! If you can beat these conditions, you're in for the trip of a lifetime! If you find yourself too far from your intended course, you might just come across the mountain's beautiful "frozen waterfall," which never melts and forms a beautiful and natural ice sculpture.

? What effect might increased tourism on this unmarked mountain have on the environment?

? What are some additional dangers that you might experience if you choose to go backcountry skiing instead of skiing down a marked slope?

Quick Fact

There are many mountains in Iran that are over 13,000 feet tall. Mount Damavand is the highest at 18,600 feet above sea level.

Skiers spend at least three days getting acclimatized to the altitude. Most people do this by skiing at a local resort.

10   9   8   7   6

WHAT GEAR WILL I NEED?

Planning a ski trip to Iran? Then check out this list of tips that explain the equipment you'll need to pack in your backpack:

SKIS: You can use your regular downhill skis and adapt your downhill bindings. But it may be better to buy lighter backcountry skis. Strapped together with a shovel and ski poles, they can become an emergency sled, if necessary.

bindings: *attachments that hold boots to skis*

SKINS: Skins are strips of fabric that fit onto the bottoms of your skis. They have hairs that lie flat when you are gliding forward, but that grip the snow to prevent you from slipping backward. Most are held onto the bottom of your skis with an adhesive. Yes, originally, skins were made of seal skin, but not anymore.

BOOTS: Your regular ski boots won't do. You will need boots with hinged ankles that will let you easily adapt from uphill climbing to downhill skiing.

POLES: Many backcountry skiers prefer ski poles that will extend for the uphill climbs and then adjust to a shorter length for downhill skiing.

SKI CRAMPONS: Sometimes you will have to climb very steep terrain and your skis, even with skins, will not work. Ski crampons attach to the bottom of your skis. They have "teeth" that grab the snow to help to stop you from slipping. They're especially good for very hard-packed or wind-affected snow.

Skiing in Iran guarantees one thing — an amazing view.

The Expert Says...

" As far as pure skiing is concerned, Iran easily holds its own compared to Europe and North America. ... Damavand is a perfect ski mountain. "

— Bob Mazarei, Swiss-based skier and magazine editor

 What do you think the expert means by pure skiing?

Take Note

Backcountry skiing in Iran is the #6 most extreme vacation on our list. Unlike regular skiing, it requires tourists to hike, climb, and ski under extreme weather conditions. Without the right equipment this vacation could end in disaster.
• Compare these conditions to exploring the active volcanoes of Ambrym. Which would you say is more extreme? Why?

Motocross racer Steve Langdon participated in the 2006 Beijing-Ulaanbaatar International Cross Country Rally across the Gobi Desert in Mongolia.

STEVE LANGDON MOTOCROSS RALLY–PHOTOS COURTESY OF SSER ORGANIZATION

RALLY

WHERE IN THE WORLD? Mongolia, in Central Asia

WOW FACTOR: This motorcycle race through the dry Gobi Desert is 2,500 miles long!

Imagine traveling under the endless blue sky of the Mongolian countryside. Now, imagine doing it as fast as you can on a motorcycle. How about trying not to fall off while racing through high mountain trails, over river crossings, and the scorching hot desert? Add the culture shock of drinking fermented horse's milk for dinner, and you're the perfect candidate to participate in the Beijing-Ulaanbaatar International Cross Country Rally. This motocross race is an incredible 2,500 miles long!

Motocross is a popular sport that means taking a motorcycle off-road through difficult terrain. If you choose to enter this race, you will be competing against some of the best riders in the world. You will do all of the navigation yourself, while you're on a bike in the middle of the desert. Then factor in the scorching 100°F temperature and you'll have an experience that will excite even the most extreme vacation junkies.

---

fermented: *not fresh; changed to a different taste by bacteria*

It's probably a good idea to bring a mechanic with you on this trip!

GETTING THERE

It's not easy getting to this location. There are few ways to get in and out of Mongolia, either by air or land. Many people in Mongolia still prefer to use horses for transportation because they are reliable and inexpensive. But don't worry. A helicopter will be on standby 24 hours a day, just in case you are in need of a rescue team.

GEARING UP

Bring your own bike, tools, and navigation gear. A support vehicle carrying camping supplies, repair equipment, food, bottled water, and fuel is provided. The Gobi Desert can actually get cold at night, so you might have to bundle up in your tent. If you decide not to bring your own mechanic along, you'll have to be prepared to do two hours of repairs at night, while other racers catch up on their sleep.

? What are some injuries that riders might be at risk of in a motocross race?

THRILL OF A LIFETIME

The total area of Mongolia is larger than Great Britain, France, Germany, and Italy combined! No wonder this is one of the longest motocross races in the world. You're going to need to get up at 4:00 AM every day to gear up! And don't expect to go to bed early. You'll be racing for eight to 15 hours every day. But don't worry — in the past, riders have been allowed a full day of rest on day six. If you love heights, this is the vacation for you. You will need to cross a mountain pass that is almost 1,000 feet high.

? What other parts of the world hold motocross races?

Riders will need to bring most of their own gear, including their own bikes and tools.

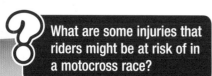

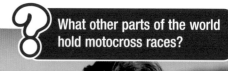

Quick Fact
The 2007 race started and ended in Ulaanbaatar, Mongolia, and not Beijing, China. China was busy preparing to host the Olympic Games in 2008.

10 9 8 7 6

Not-So-Easy Rider

Motocross rider Steve Langdon took part in the 2006 Beijing-Ulaanbaatar International Cross Country Rally. In these quotations, he recalls the danger he faced in Mongolia.

" I spotted a cloud of dust about two kilometers [over one mile] off and beelined it cross country. Concentrating on not hitting the rock-hard camel grass, I didn't notice the dried-up riverbed fast approaching. I blipped the throttle but landed in a pile of loose rock. "

" In the middle of the Gobi Desert, the mid-day temperature was 40°C [100°F] and the only shade available was under the fuel truck. So about 10 of us sought refuge under this old ... truck and ate our lunch. "

beelined: *went straight to*
blipped: *made a quick, jerking movement*
throttle: *device to control flow of fuel to engine*

" I had another mishap, this time with a washed-out culvert, obscured by clouds of dust. I tried to get myself and my bike out of the way to avoid getting run over by the other riders, but the bike would not start; the main fuse had blown. "

culvert: *part of land that passes over a sewer or drain*

The Expert Says...

" Motorcycling has enhanced my life like you cannot believe and it has nothing to do with the money — if you let it, it's like magic. "

— Lawrence Hacking, 2005 participant in the Beijing-Ulaanbaatar International Cross Country Rally

? What does Lawrence Hacking mean by "if you let it, it's like magic." Can you say this of any sport you have tried? Explain.

Take Note

This motorcycle race speeds in at #5 on our list. Like climbing to the top of a ski mountain in Iran, tourists must have excellent navigational skills if they want to survive. Mongolia's remote location is ideal for thrill-seekers, but without the right tools they could find themselves far away from the finish line.
• Compare the types of skills that a tourist would need for this trip with those needed for backcountry skiing in Iran. What additional arguments can you make for this vacation being ranked at #5?

5   4   3   2   1

4 ADVENTURE

Travelers don't have to choose only one sport in this race. Hiking, swimming, and cycling might all be necessary skills.

MOUNTAIN BIKING—MARK A. JOHNSON/CORBIS

RACING

WHERE IN THE WORLD? Anywhere extreme! It could be up in the mountains, down a river filled with rapids, or deep in the rain forest.

WOW FACTOR: These outdoor races can last for days and combine up to a half-dozen sports into one exhausting competition.

Do you think that the danger and excitement of extreme sports are for you, but you can't decide on just one sport? Well, then you're the perfect candidate for an adventure race. This extreme vacation is the ideal challenge for those who want to see the world, while trying to outrun, out-boat, or out-bike their competition. These races can combine any number of extreme sports. And you don't have to do it alone. You will do it as part of a team.

But don't sign up just yet! This vacation isn't for just anyone. Teams must be willing to climb to great heights, raft through dangerous waters, and bike ride across jagged terrain. And don't forget about the risk of poisonous snakebites, extreme weather conditions, and exhausting physical activity.

Adventure racing is an intense battle to the finish line. May the best team win!

ADVENTURE RACING

GETTING THERE

Unlike other excursions in this book, adventure racing can take place almost anywhere in the world! If you choose to go, you must be willing to leave the industrialized world behind. You will never know what to expect when you step off the plane. Adventure racers will embark on a journey through thick jungles, down roaring rapids, and across terrifying cliffs! Some popular races are held in New Zealand, Australia, and Canada. Some even require traveling to hidden, unmapped territory that few people have ever seen before.

> Why do you think that racers are willing to spend months training intensely for only a few days of racing?

GEARING UP

If you are serious about joining an adventure expedition, you'd better work at getting in shape, or you could end up badly injured. Travelers who sign up usually have experience in many sports such as running, kayaking, and cycling. Much of the equipment you will need is provided, but you might want to bring your own inline skates or bicycle, especially if they have been specially made to fit your body. And don't forget your compass. Getting lost on an isolated trail could cost you the race — or worse!

kayaking: *traveling by lightweight canoe*

Quick Fact

Television producers realized that this extreme vacation would make exciting television. Between 1995 and 2002, millions of viewers tuned in to watch *Eco-Challenge*. This exciting reality television show followed teams of four as they raced more than 300 miles, 24 hours a day.

THRILL OF A LIFETIME

Adventure races aren't your typical race to the finish line. Only the toughest and bravest competitors can make it to the end. Racers need to be physically fit. They often go for days with limited sleep and little food, and they face unpredictable weather conditions while scaling great heights and swimming in deep waters. Many adventure races are so tough that some racers don't complete their trek. However, the experience of navigating coastal rain forests, sandy beaches, and rocky cliffs still makes adventure racing an unforgettable experience!

> If you were designing an adventure race, what sports or activities would you include?

In some adventure races, teams must face whitewater rapids to get to the finish line.

AN AMAZING RACE

Are you adventurous? Do you have a competitive edge? Check out this chart for some of the most extreme adventure races around the world.

RACE	TEAM	LENGTH	ENTRY FEE	SKILLS
Southern Traverse, New Zealand	Teams of two or four	Three days with rests	around $500 per competitor	trekking, mountain biking, kayaking, map-reading
GeoQuest 48-Hour Adventure Race, Australia	Teams of four	48 hours nonstop	around $400 per competitor	trekking, mountain biking kayaking, navigation
MIchigan eXpedition Adventure Race, Michigan, USA	Teams of four	Four days nonstop	around $2,500 per team	trekking, kayaking, canoeing, mountain biking
Raid the North Extreme, British Columbia, Canada	Teams of four	Six days nonstop	around $4,500 per team	trekking, mountain biking, paddling, mountain climbing, navigation

The Expert Says...

" Adventure racing is the most addictive sport you will ever try, and once you get sucked in, there's no going back. "

— Robyn Benincasa, *Florida Sports Magazine*

Take Note

Adventure racing expeditions cross the finish line at #4. Unlike motocross racing, you will be working with a team on this adventure. Depending on your team members, this might help you or put you behind as you deal with bad weather conditions and challenging terrain.

- Compare the benefits of working alone and working with a team. Which do you think would be better? Why?

5 4 3 2 1

This underwater vacation might be beautiful, but it can also be deadly. Equipment failure is possible and can mean sudden death.

WHERE IN THE WORLD? Parts of Antarctica, including the South Shetland Islands and Deception Island

WOW FACTOR: You'll be immersed in freezing cold water, with only your breathing equipment keeping you from drowning.

Imagine sliding beneath the ocean's icy surface, with only your breathing apparatus and dry suit to protect you from the frigid cold. One leak or small puncture in your suit and your body will fall into a state of severe shock. After only a few minutes, anyone unprotected here will be fatally overcome with hypothermia. For this reason, only the brave and the adventurous will dive into this water!

Once host only to scientists and explorers, the South Shetland Islands, Deception Island, and the bays and channels of Antarctica have become tourist haunts for extreme diving fanatics. But don't book your ticket just yet. Even if you have passed a basic scuba diving course and completed open water dives, you're still not qualified to conquer these waters. Divers must have advanced qualifications such as experience with deep diving, night diving, wreck diving, and underwater navigation.

Do you think you're brave enough? Then it's time to dive into our #3 extreme vacation!

apparatus: *equipment*
hypothermia: *dangerously low body temperature*

ICE DIVING

GETTING THERE

Depending on how much you want to pay, ship accommodations range from lavish to basic. Lightweight, inflatable boats will take you from your vessel to the perfect spot from which to dive. In some cases, the ice is too thick for boats to pass, so large drills are used to tunnel through the icy surface. This process creates holes for divers to pass through.

> **?** What are some reasons that travelers might decide on an underwater vacation instead of staying on land?

GEARING UP

Breathing regulators can easily fail in these extreme temperatures, so you'll need to bring two that are designed especially for the cold! Make sure to pack a lot of warm clothing. You'll need it! This includes at least two sets of thermal underwear, dry gloves, and an ice cap, which is a piece of clothing worn to keep your head warm. All this equipment will not come cheap either.

lavish: *luxurious; extravagant*

> **?** How do you think breathing regulators function in such cold temperatures? Check it out.

A diver floats upside down under ice.

THRILL OF A LIFETIME

Once you're suited up properly, you're ready to dive! You will never forget the amazing ice formations and the spectacular range of colors underneath the ocean's surface. You'll have an up-close view of hundreds of unique sea and land creatures, including seals, whales, and penguins, to name only a few. Beautiful walls of ice will tower over you. But stay close to your guide! Shifting ice makes it easy to lose your way.

Quick Fact

Believe it or not, experts don't recommend using new equipment when ice diving. Divers should use equipment that they have brought on previous dives so they are comfortable with how to use it properly.

A diver prepares for ice diving.

10   9   8   7   6

Lair of the Leopards

In this article from *Diver* magazine, Yvette Cardozo describes the amazing sights she saw on her icy dives.

Leopard seals aren't known to be violent, but anything can happen.

We were so entranced by the wall of … ice at our fingertips that we never saw the dark shadow behind us. Slowly, it grew closer. … One of the divers happened to turn round, and there, just inches from his mask, was a set of furry nostrils.

It was a leopard seal, and it wasn't our first. The seals had been with us almost from the moment we hit the water. …

Leopard seals get their name from their spots — and their viciously predatory nature. But they eat penguins, not people — at least, not usually. …

But no one expected the leopard seals, or the sheer beauty of the ice, not to mention the brilliant topside scenery. …

Penguins swam twitchily across the glass-smooth water. Behind all this, walls of square-cut ice rose in cracked columns that avalanched regularly, sometimes bringing down a 30 meter-wide [100-feet] face.

entranced: *carried away with wonder*

As the setting sun turned all this snow gold and then pink … three humpback whales floated.

They blew clouds of fishy breath our way and rumbled like elephants. They were so close that we could count the bumps on their noses. …

Our [next] ice dive was at Pleneau Island, in a graveyard of ice chunks. Some were bigger than houses, but grounded, so there was no danger of them rolling onto us. … [W]e anchored next to one, dropped into the water and slid to the bottom at 25 meters [80 feet]. …

And of course, there was the leopard seal. He spiraled out and up, then back in, twisting and circling around us. …

Could it get any better? Well, yes. Just as we surfaced, two penguins torpedoed by, leaping out of the water and bouncing, like so many skipping stones.

The Expert Says…

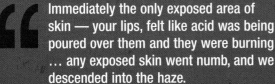

" Immediately the only exposed area of skin — your lips, felt like acid was being poured over them and they were burning … any exposed skin went numb, and we descended into the haze. "

— Tony Davis, owner of the company Aqua Tech Australia

Take Note

This icy adventure ranks #3. Of all the vacations described so far, ice diving places tourists at greatest risk of losing their oxygen. Loss of oxygen causes divers' reactions to be slower, placing them at greater risk when in danger.
• Compare this adventure with other vacations in which lack of oxygen may pose a danger. Which do you think is the riskiest vacation?

5   4   3   2   1

2 DIVING TO THE

Few people have ever seen the world's most famous shipwreck up close, nearly a century after it sank to the bottom of the Atlantic.

RESTING PLACE OF THE TITANIC—WALDEN MEDIA/KPA–ZUMA/KEYSTONE

TITANIC

WHERE IN THE WORLD? Almost 400 miles off the coast of Newfoundland, 12,500 feet beneath the Atlantic Ocean

WOW FACTOR: There is no turning back once you're inside a tight, confined submersible at the bottom of the ocean.

Imagine that you are plunging 100 feet a minute into the dark abyss of the North Atlantic. Far below the murky surface lies the ghostly wreck of the *Titanic*. Only a handful of people have ever had the chance to embark on this costly and extreme vacation.

This adventure is not for the faint of heart. Intense water pressure at the bottom of the ocean is enough to crush an average submarine. For this reason, you'll travel more than two miles to the ocean floor in a small MIR submersible, so you'd better not be claustrophobic.

If that doesn't sound scary enough, consider the fact that you'll be traveling in complete darkness! There is no light after you've descended 800 feet, except for the glow of phosphorescent plankton. Not until the pilot turns on the lights do the bones of the broken ship and its spilled contents come into view. Your small submersible will look tiny beside the hull of this monstrous ship.

Once you've reached this underwater gravesite, you might see broken plates, shoes, and other evidence of the 1,500 lives that were lost on April 15, 1912. If you think that being this close to history is worth an extreme $45,000 price tag, then climb aboard your MIR for this haunting vacation!

MIR submersible: *vessel used for underwater research*
claustrophobic: *fear of being in a tight, enclosed space*
phosphorescent: *able to give off light*

DIVING TO THE TITANIC

The MIR submersible is hoisted into the water via a cable connected to the ship.

GETTING THERE

Before leaving for this extreme vacation, the first thing to do is to have a medical screening. Only the healthy will be able to travel — it's not easy to find a doctor when you're thousands of feet underwater! On your way to the dive site, you will spend a few days on a comfortable ship that conducts research. Here you will meet explorers, scientists, and the submersible pilots who will be with you on your trip. It took researchers nearly 75 years to locate the resting place of the *Titanic*. You'll be there in less than a day!

GEARING UP

You won't need to pack too much for this trip, but warm clothes are a must! The middle of the Atlantic can be frigid, no matter what time of the year you are traveling! No dive experience is necessary, so you can leave your oxygen tank and diving gear at home.

> **?** Do you think that the experience of diving to the *Titanic* is worth the expensive price tag? Explain.

> **Quick Fact**
>
> The MIRs are two of only five submersibles in the world capable of operating at depths of over 9,840 feet. They were used to film underwater scenes for the movie *Titanic*.

THRILL OF A LIFETIME

Imagine staring at the world's most famous shipwreck with only a seven-inch acrylic port standing between you and the powerful depths of the Atlantic. This isn't just a quick stop at the bottom of the ocean! Travelers spend 11 to 12 hours exploring the ship's enormous boilers, propellers, and rusting metal. This amazing view is one that is usually reserved for scientists and historians!

port: *round, window-like opening*

> **?** Some people consider the wreck of the *Titanic* a gravesite and think that it should not be visited by tourists. Do you agree? Explain.

It took almost 75 years to locate the wreck of the Titanic.

Dive to *Titanic's* Watery Grave for only $45,000

ATTENTION THRILL-SEEKERS! FOR ONLY $45,000 YOU COULD BE THE NEXT TRAVELER TO CRUISE ALONGSIDE THE WORLD'S MOST FAMOUS SHIPWRECK. READ THIS BROCHURE TO FIND OUT MORE.

Your round-trip ticket to the depths of the Atlantic Ocean will include:

- One night's accommodation in beautiful Newfoundland, Canada
- Accommodation aboard the *Akademik Keldysh*, a comfortable research vessel
- Meals that are prepared by a world-class chef
- One seat on a MIR submersible, on its way to the *Titanic's* final resting place
- A deep-ocean dive 12,500 feet below land, which lasts 11 to 12 hours
- A clear view of *Titanic's* huge anchors, propellers, famous bridge, and what remains of the once magnificent grand staircase
- Glimpses of the ship's very personal history, such as passenger luggage, plates, and shoes

The **Titanic** *rests underwater.*

WARNING: Proof of medical tests will be required before embarking on this extreme vacation. Passengers with heart problems, arthritis, seizure disorders, claustrophobia, or severe asthma will not be permitted to dive.

The Expert Says...

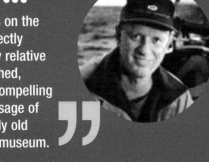

" When you see pairs of shoes on the bottom of the ocean ... perfectly preserved and sitting exactly relative to the body that's now vanished, those ... are a much more compelling message — a personal message of tragedy — than some wrinkly old shoes sitting on a shelf in a museum. "

— Robert Ballard, person who discovered the *Titanic* 73 years after it sank

Take Note

If breathing is difficult when ice diving under only a few feet of icy water, imagine what would happen if your submersible sprang a leak at a depth of almost 12,500 feet. The high risks associated with this extreme vacation, along with the hefty price tag, place this historic dive at #2 on our list.

- Compare this adventure with ice diving. Which trip do you think is more dangerous? Give reasons for your answer.

5   4   3   **2**   1

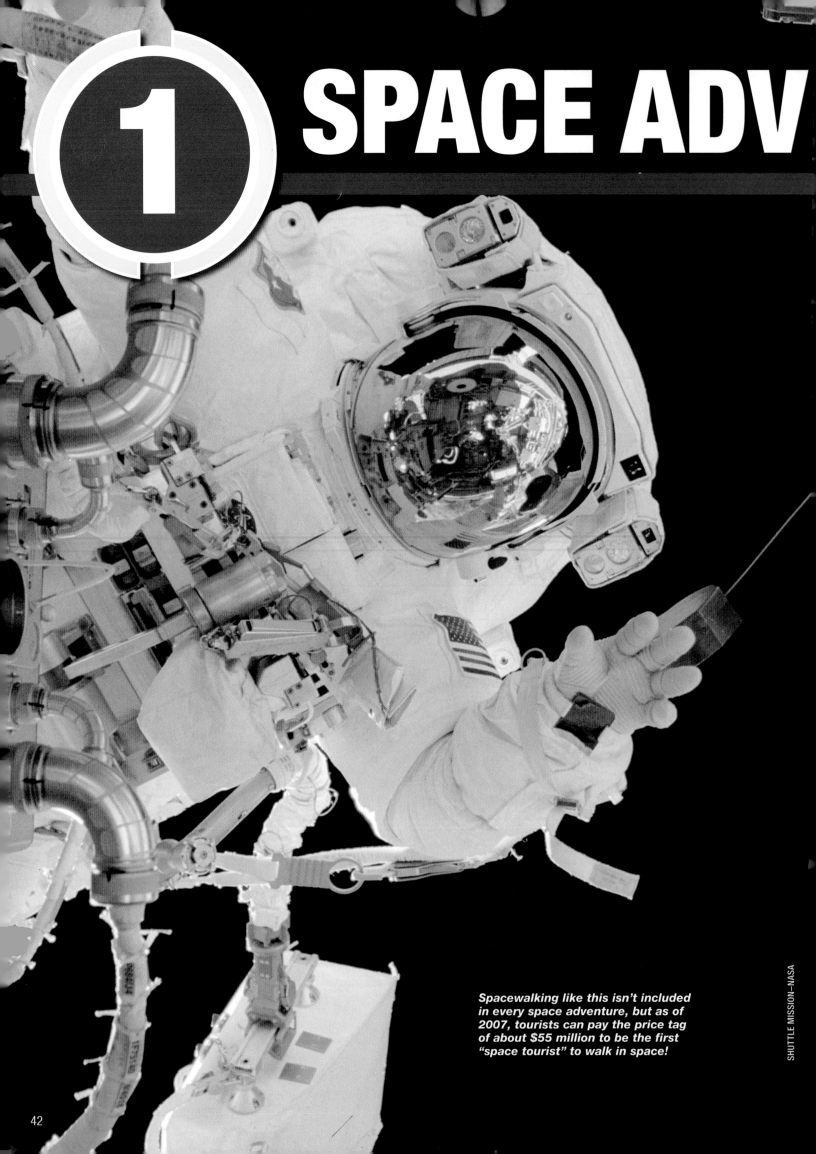

Spacewalking like this isn't included in every space adventure, but as of 2007, tourists can pay the price tag of about $55 million to be the first "space tourist" to walk in space!

SHUTTLE MISSION—NASA

ENTURE

WHERE IN THE WORLD? It's out of this world!

WOW FACTOR: Fewer than 500 human beings have been this far away from the planet. Only a few of these have been space tourists!

Imagine that you are strapped into a spaceship and hurled upward into the great unknown! You will be powerless as four times the force of gravity shakes your sturdy spaceship. In your own specially made spacesuit, your knees will be pressed to your chest in the tiny capsule. In less than 15 minutes, you'll be orbiting Earth at a speed of more than 16,000 miles an hour.

You can't get more adventurous than this! Everything from the intense training to the cost of this vacation is out of this world. You can expect to pay a cool $25 million to leave Earth. But being a millionaire doesn't mean that you will have what it takes! You'll need to prove yourself in a challenging space training program before you're allowed to blast off.

SPACE ADVENTURE

GETTING THERE

You can't blast off to the International Space Station before you're trained to use all the gadgets of spaceflight. First you will train in a *centrifuge* to learn how the body reacts to increased gravity. Once you blast off from Earth, it will be 30 hours before your spaceship locks onto the International Space Station. You will look back at the world from an incredible 200 miles away! For just a split second, you will smell "burnt cookies" as you transfer to the space station. This is what space travelers recall as being the "smell of outer space." Once you arrive, you will spend your eight to 14 days of vacation aboard the station in complete weightlessness!

GEARING UP

You won't need to do much packing for this extreme vacation. All of the gear you need will be provided. First you'll need to know how to move around in your spacesuit. This means you will take spacesuit training, spacewalk *simulation* training, International Space Station simulator training, space navigation training, and land survival training. You'll even board an airplane called a MiG-25 and fly to the edge of space with an experienced pilot for practice. If you can withstand this extreme training, then you're ready to go!

centrifuge: *module that simulates traveling in a spacecraft*
simulation: *imitating the real experience*

THRILL OF A LIFETIME

Settling in for several days of life aboard the space station isn't as easy as you might think! You will have to relearn everything from your body movements to eating and drinking. Everything will seem different when you can't put two feet on the ground! The space station is even equipped with water, microwave ovens, and refrigerators so you can eat normal "Earth-like" meals. When it's time to leave, you'll spend a dramatic four hours plummeting downward toward Earth.

? As technology improves, how do you think space travel will change in the future?

As of 2007, five space tourists have visited the International Space Station.

Quick Fact

The building of the International Space Station started in 1998. It is the third brightest object in the night sky after the moon and Venus.

The Expert Says...

"Quite simply, there is nothing as beautiful as the Earth seen from space — it is absolutely breathtaking."

— Mark Shuttleworth, space tourism participant

Anousheh Ansari's blog from space

Anousheh Ansari is the first female space tourist. While in space, she was able to keep in touch with her fans and family through a space blog. Read these excerpts to learn more about her extreme vacation.

September 17, 2006

I'm hours away from my flight ...

I just want to get the launch behind me and start floating in the wonderful weightlessness of space. ... It feels like waiting in a doctor's office for the test results. ...

September 27, 2006

Being in weightlessness has its wonderful advantages. ...

In space it is okay to play with your food. ... The cheese puffs are not put into the mouth by hand, they are slightly jolted out of the container and flown to your mouth. When you open a bag of soft food like yogurt or soup, if you are not really, really careful, small yogurt bubbles or soup bubbles start floating around and then you can catch them with your spoon. ...

 Even though Anousheh had Internet access in space, what are some of the comforts of Earth that she would have had to do without on this trip?

September 28, 2006

I'm writing my last blog from orbit. It is a bittersweet feeling. ...

I was also just talking to my sister and I could hear in her voice how anxious she was and how scared she was of losing me ... I promised her that I will be fine and will be with her in a few days ... I could tell she was crying but trying hard not to let it show in her voice.

September 30, 2006

I'm back on our beautiful Earth. ...

It was a difficult day for me and from the moment I opened my eyes I had butterflies in my stomach. ...

We hit the ground so hard I thought we were buried in the dirt but then we had a little bounce and rolled to one side. ... I felt like a million needles were pushed in my back and felt an intense pain. ...

My journey had ended but my quest to open up the gates to the universe for everyone else has just begun.

Take Note

This extreme adventure zooms into the #1 spot. Like the *Titanic* adventure, this is a journey into previously unreachable territory. Travelers on both trips face astronomical risks. However, while the traveler is just an observer on the trip to the *Titanic*, the space traveler is an active participant who has to undergo intense training in order to survive in space and to perform space-related activities, such as scientific experiments.
• If money were no object, would you hop aboard this space adventure? Why or why not?

MONITOR–SHUTTERSTOCK; ALL OTHER IMAGES–NASA

5   4   3   2   **1**

We Thought ...

Here are the criteria we used in ranking the 10 most extreme vacations.

The vacation:
- Can be risky and dangerous
- Requires a great amount of bravery
- Takes incredible skills or endurance
- Has not been done by many people
- Is to a unique, often unmapped, location
- Requires training and physical conditioning before the trip
- Means surviving dangerous terrain
- Requires special equipment
- Is one that won't be easily forgotten

What Do You Think?

1. Do you agree with our ranking? If you don't, try ranking these vacations yourself. Justify your ranking with data from your own research and reasoning. You may refer to our criteria, or you may want to draw up your own list of criteria.

2. Here are three other extreme vacations that did not make the list: rafting through the Ruakuri Caves, a dogsled safari in Northwest Lapland, and diving with great white sharks in South Africa.
   • Find out more about these vacations. Do you think they should have made our list? Give reasons for your response.
   • Are there other vacations that you think should have made our list? Explain your choices.

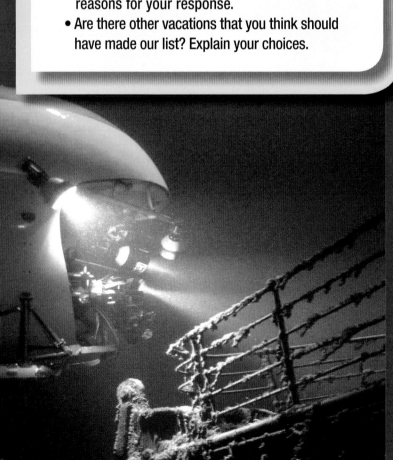

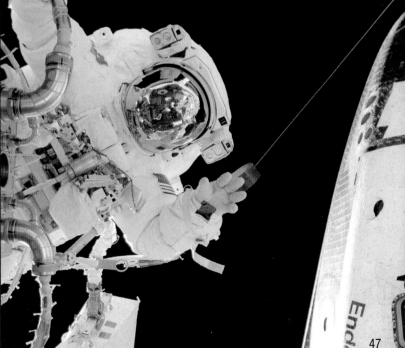

Index